December, A Month In Verse

Poetry is a fascinating use of language. With almost a million words at its command it is not surprising that these Isles have produced some of the most beautiful, moving and descriptive verse through the centuries. In this series we look at each calendar month through the eyes and minds of our most gifted poets to bring you a guide to the days within each . This volume of Poetry is all about **December** - The 12th and final month in the Gregorian calendar. Winter is upon the land and Christmas provides a source of celebration. The poets including such notables as John Keats, Lord Byron, William Shakespeare, Percy Bsysshe Shelley, Alfred Lord Tennyson reflect their views and extend their thoughts to us. Among our readers are Richard Mitchley and Ghizela Rowe

Many samples are at our youtube channel
http://www.youtube.com/user/PortablePoetry?feature=mhee Among the readers are Richard Mitchley and Ghizela Rowe The full volume can be purchased from iTunes, Amazon and other digital stores.

INDEX OF POEMS

Ode Written On The First Of December by Robert Southey

Tho' now no more the musing ear
Delights to listen to the breeze
That lingers o'er the green wood shade,
I love thee Winter! well.

Sweet are the harmonies of Spring,
Sweet is the summer's evening gale,
Pleasant the autumnal winds that shake
The many-colour'd grove.

And pleasant to the sober'd soul
The silence of the wintry scene,
When Nature shrouds her in her trance

Not undelightful now to roam
The wild heath sparkling on the sight;
Not undelightful now to pace
The forest's ample rounds;

And see the spangled branches shine,
And mark the moss of many a hue
That varies the old tree's brown bark,
Or o'er the grey stone spreads.

The cluster'd berries claim the eye
O'er the bright hollies gay green leaves,
The ivy round the leafless oak
Clasps its full foliage close.

So virtue diffident of strength
Clings to religion's firmer aid,
And by religion's aid upheld
Endures calamity.

Nor void of beauties now the spring,
Whose waters hid from summer sun
Have sooth'd the thirsty pilgrim's ear
With more than melody.

The green moss shines with icey glare,
The long grass bends its spear-like form,
And lovely is the silvery scene
When faint the sunbeams smile.

Reflection too may love the hour
When Nature, hid in Winter's grave,
No more expands the bursting bud
Or bids the flowret bloom.

For Nature soon in Spring's best charms
Shall rise reviv'd from Winter's grave.
Again expand the bursting bud,
And bid the flowret bloom.

A Calender Of Sonnets - December by Helen Hunt Jackson
The lakes of ice gleam bluer than the lakes
Of water 'neath the summer sunshine gleamed:
Far fairer than when placidly it streamed,
The brook its frozen architecture makes,
And under bridges white its swift way takes.
Snow comes and goes as messenger who dreamed
Might linger on the road; or one who deemed
His message hostile gently for their sakes
Who listened might reveal it by degrees.
We gird against the cold of winter wind
Our loins now with mighty bands of sleep,
In longest, darkest nights take rest and ease,
And every shortening day, as shadows creep
O'er the brief noontide, fresh surprises find.

A December Day by Robert Fuller Murray
Blue, blue is the sea to-day,
Warmly the light
Sleeps on St. Andrews Bay
Blue, fringed with white.

That's no December sky!
Surely 'tis June
Holds now her state on high,
Queen of the noon.

Only the tree-tops bare
Crowning the hill,
Clear-cut in perfect air,
Warn us that still

Winter, the aged chief,
Mighty in power,
Exiles the tender leaf,
Exiles the flower.

Is there a heart to-day,
A heart that grieves
For flowers that fade away,
For fallen leaves?

Oh, not in leaves or flowers
Endures the charm
That clothes those naked towers

With love-light warm.

O dear St. Andrews Bay,
Winter or Spring
Gives not nor takes away
Memories that cling

All round thy girdling reefs,
That walk thy shore,
Memories of joys and griefs
Ours evermore.

A Wife In London (December 1899) by Thomas Hardy
I The Tragedy
She sits in the tawny vapour
That the City lanes have uprolled,
Behind whose webby fold on fold
Like a waning taper
The street-lamp glimmers cold.

A messenger's knock cracks smartly,
Flashed news is in her hand
Of meaning it dazes to understand
Though shaped so shortly:
He--has fallen--in the far South Land

II The Irony
'Tis the morrow; the fog hangs thicker,
The postman nears and goes:
A letter is brought whose lines disclose
By the firelight flicker
His hand, whom the worm now knows:

Fresh--firm--penned in highest feather -
Page-full of his hoped return,
And of home-planned jaunts by brake and burn
In the summer weather,
And of new love that they would learn.

Come Come Thou Bleak December Wind (Fragment 3) by Samuel Taylor Coleridge
Come, come thou bleak December wind,
And blow the dry leaves from the tree!
Flash, like a Love-thought, thro' me, Death
And take a Life that wearies me.

Snow-Bound (The Sun That Brief December Day) by John Greenleaf Whittier

The sun that brief December day
Rose cheerless over hills of gray,
And, darkly circled, gave at noon
A sadder light than waning moon.
Slow tracing down the thickening sky
Its mute and ominous prophecy,
A portent seeming less than threat,
It sank from sight before it set.
A chill no coat, however stout,
Of homespun stuff could quite shut out,
A hard, dull bitterness of cold,
That checked, mid-vein, the circling race
Of life-blood in the sharpened face,
The coming of the snow-storm told.
The wind blew east; we heard the roar
Of Ocean on his wintry shore,
And felt the strong pulse throbbing there
Beat with low rhythm our inland air.

Meanwhile we did our nightly chores,
Brought in the wood from out of doors,
Littered the stalls, and from the mows
Raked down the herd's-grass for the cows;
Heard the horse whinnying for his corn;
And, sharply clashing horn on horn,
Impatient down the stanchion rows
The cattle shake their walnut bows;
While, peering from his early perch
Upon the scaffold's pole of birch,
The cock his crested helmet bent
And down his querulous challenge sent.

Unwarmed by any sunset light
The gray day darkened into night,
A night made hoary with the swarm
And whirl-dance of the blinding storm,
As zigzag, wavering to and fro,
Crossed and recrossed the wingëd snow:
And ere the early bedtime came
The white drift piled the window-frame,
And through the glass the clothes-line posts
Looked in like tall and sheeted ghosts.

So all night long the storm roared on:
The morning broke without a sun;
In tiny spherule traced with lines
Of Nature's geometric signs,
In starry flake, and pellicle,
All day the hoary meteor fell;
And, when the second morning shone,
We looked upon a world unknown,
On nothing we could call our own.

Around the glistening wonder bent
The blue walls of the firmament,
No cloud above, no earth below,
A universe of sky and snow!
The old familiar sights of ours
Took marvellous shapes; strange domes and towers
Rose up where sty or corn-crib stood,
Or garden-wall, or belt of wood;
A smooth white mound the brush-pile showed,
A fenceless drift what once was road;
The bridle-post an old man sat
With loose-flung coat and high cocked hat;
The well-curb had a Chinese roof;
And even the long sweep, high aloof,
In its slant spendor, seemed to tell
Of Pisa's leaning miracle.

A prompt, decisive man, no breath
Our father wasted: "Boys, a path!"
Well pleased, (for when did farmer boy
Count such a summons less than joy?)
Our buskins on our feet we drew;
With mittened hands, and caps drawn low,
To guard our necks and ears from snow,
We cut the solid whiteness through.
And, where the drift was deepest, made
A tunnel walled and overlaid
With dazzling crystal: we had read
Of rare Aladdin's wondrous cave,
And to our own his name we gave,
With many a wish the luck were ours
To test his lamp's supernal powers.
We reached the barn with merry din,
And roused the prisoned brutes within.
The old horse thrust his long head out,
And grave with wonder gazed about;
The cock his lusty greeting said,
And forth his speckled harem led;
The oxen lashed their tails, and hooked,
And mild reproach of hunger looked;
The hornëd patriarch of the sheep,
Like Egypt's Amun roused from sleep,
Shook his sage head with gesture mute,
And emphasized with stamp of foot.

All day the gusty north-wind bore
The loosening drift its breath before;
Low circling round its southern zone,
The sun through dazzling snow-mist shone.
No church-bell lent its Christian tone
To the savage air, no social smoke
Curled over woods of snow-hung oak.

A solitude made more intense
By dreary-voicëd elements,
The shrieking of the mindless wind,
The moaning tree-boughs swaying blind,
And on the glass the unmeaning beat
Of ghostly finger-tips of sleet.
Beyond the circle of our hearth
No welcome sound of toil or mirth
Unbound the spell, and testified
Of human life and thought outside.
We minded that the sharpest ear
The buried brooklet could not hear,
The music of whose liquid lip
Had been to us companionship,
And, in our lonely life, had grown
To have an almost human tone.

As night drew on, and, from the crest
Of wooded knolls that ridged the west,
The sun, a snow-blown traveller, sank
From sight beneath the smothering bank,
We piled, with care, our nightly stack
Of wood against the chimney-back,
The oaken log, green, huge, and thick,
And on its top the stout back-stick;
The knotty forestick laid apart,
And filled between with curious art
The ragged brush; then, hovering near,
We watched the first red blaze appear,
Heard the sharp crackle, caught the gleam
On whitewashed wall and sagging beam,
Until the old, rude-furnished room
Burst, flower-like, into rosy bloom;
While radiant with a mimic flame
Outside the sparkling drift became,
And through the bare-boughed lilac-tree
Our own warm hearth seemed blazing free.
The crane and pendent trammels showed,
The Turks' heads on the andirons glowed;
While childish fancy, prompt to tell
The meaning of the miracle,
Whispered the old rhyme: "Under the tree,
When fire outdoors burns merrily,
There the witches are making tea."

The moon above the eastern wood
Shone at its full; the hill-range stood
Transfigured in the silver flood,
Its blown snows flashing cold and keen,
Dead white, save where some sharp ravine
Took shadow, or the sombre green
Of hemlocks turned to pitchy black

Against the whiteness at their back.
For such a world and such a night
Most fitting that unwarming light,
Which only seemed where'er it fell
To make the coldness visible.

Shut in from all the world without,
We sat the clean-winged hearth about,
Content to let the north-wind roar
In baffled rage at pane and door,
While the red logs before us beat
The frost-line back with tropic heat;
And ever, when a louder blast
Shook beam and rafter as it passed,
The merrier up its roaring draught
The great throat of the chimney laughed;
The house-dog on his paws outspread
Laid to the fire his drowsy head,
The cat's dark silhouette on the wall
A couchant tiger's seemed to fall;
And, for the winter fireside meet,
Between the andirons' straddling feet,
The mug of cider simmered slow,
The apples sputtered in a row,
And, close at hand, the basket stood
With nuts from brown October's wood.

What matter how the night behaved?
What matter how the north-wind raved?
Blow high, blow low, not all its snow
Could quench our hearth-fire's ruddy glow.
O Time and Change!—with hair as gray
As was my sire's that winter day,
How strange it seems, with so much gone
Of life and love, to still live on!
Ah, brother! only I and thou
Are left of all that circle now,
The dear home faces whereupon
That fitful firelight paled and shone.
Henceforward, listen as we will,
The voices of that hearth are still;
Look where we may, the wide earth o'er,
Those lighted faces smile no more.
We tread the paths their feet have worn,
We sit beneath their orchard trees,
We hear, like them, the hum of bees
And rustle of the bladed corn;
We turn the pages that they read,
Their written words we linger o'er,
But in the sun they cast no shade,
No voice is heard, no sign is made,
No step is on the conscious floor!

Yet Love will dream, and Faith will trust,
(Since He who knows our need is just,)
That somehow, somewhere, meet we must.
Alas for him who never sees
The stars shine through his cypress-trees!
Who, hopeless, lays his dead away,
Nor looks to see the breaking day
Across the mournful marbles play!
Who hath not learned, in hours of faith,
The truth to flesh and sense unknown,
That Life is ever lord of Death,
And Love can never lose its own!
We sped the time with stories old,
Wrought puzzles out, and riddles told,
Or stammered from our school-book lore
"The Chief of Gambia's golden shore."
How often since, when all the land
Was clay in Slavery's shaping hand,
As if a far-blown trumpet stirred
The languorous sin-sick air, I heard:
"Does not the voice of reason cry,
Claim the first right which Nature gave,
From the red scourge of bondage to fly,
Nor deign to live a burdened slave!"
Our father rode again his ride
On Memphremagog's wooded side;
Sat down again to moose and samp
In trapper's hut and Indian camp;
Lived o'er the old idyllic ease
Beneath St. François' hemlock-trees;
Again for him the moonlight shone
On Norman cap and bodiced zone;
Again he heard the violin play
Which led the village dance away.
And mingled in its merry whirl
The grandam and the laughing girl.
Or, nearer home, our steps he led
Where Salisbury's level marshes spread
Mile-wide as flies the laden bee;
Where merry mowers, hale and strong,
Swept, scythe on scythe, their swaths along
The low green prairies of the sea.
We shared the fishing off Boar's Head,
And round the rocky Isles of Shoals
The hake-broil on the drift-wood coals;
The chowder on the sand-beach made,
Dipped by the hungry, steaming hot,
With spoons of clam-shell from the pot.
We heard the tales of witchcraft old,
And dream and sign and marvel told
To sleepy listeners as they lay
Stretched idly on the salted hay,

Adrift along the winding shores,
When favoring breezes deigned to blow
The square sail of the gundelow
And idle lay the useless oars.

Our mother, while she turned her wheel
Or run the new-knit stocking-heel,
Told how the Indian hordes came down
At midnight on Concheco town,
And how her own great-uncle bore
His cruel scalp-mark to fourscore.
Recalling, in her fitting phrase,
So rich and picturesque and free
(The common unrhymed poetry
Of simple life and country ways,)
The story of her early days,
She made us welcome to her home;
Old hearths grew wide to give us room;
We stole with her a frightened look
At the gray wizard's conjuring-book,
The fame whereof went far and wide
Through all the simple country side;
We heard the hawks at twilight play,
The boat-horn on Piscataqua,
The loon's weird laughter far away;
We fished her little trout-brook, knew
What flowers in wood and meadow grew,
What sunny hillsides autumn-brown
She climbed to shake the ripe nuts down,
Saw where in sheltered cove and bay,
The ducks' black squadron anchored lay,
And heard the wild-geese calling loud
Beneath the gray November cloud.

Then, haply, with a look more grave,
And soberer tone, some tale she gave
From painful Sewel's ancient tome,
Beloved in every Quaker home,
Of faith fire-winged by martyrdom,
Or Chalkley's Journal, old and quaint,
Gentlest of skippers, rare sea-saint!
Who, when the dreary calms prevailed,
And water-butt and bread-cask failed,
And cruel, hungry eyes pursued
His portly presence mad for food,
With dark hints muttered under breath
Of casting lots for life or death,
Offered, if Heaven withheld supplies,
To be himself the sacrifice.
Then, suddenly, as if to save
The good man from his living grave,
A ripple on the water grew,

A school of porpoise flashed in view.
"Take, eat," he said, "and be content;
These fishes in my stead are sent
By Him who gave the tangled ram
To spare the child of Abraham."

Our uncle, innocent of books,
Was rich in lore of fields and brooks,
The ancient teachers never dumb
Of Nature's unhoused lyceum.
In moons and tides and weather wise,
He read the clouds as prophecies,
And foul or fair could well divine,
By many an occult hint and sign,
Holding the cunning-warded keys
To all the woodcraft mysteries;
Himself to Nature's heart so near
That all her voices in his ear
Of beast or bird had meanings clear,
Like Apollonius of old,
Who knew the tales the sparrows told,
Or Hermes, who interpreted
What the sage cranes of Nilus said;
A simple, guileless, childlike man,
Content to live where life began;
Strong only on his native grounds,
The little world of sights and sounds
Whose girdle was the parish bounds,
Whereof his fondly partial pride
The common features magnified,
As Surrey hills to mountains grew
In White of Selborne's loving view,
He told how teal and loon he shot,
And how the eagle's eggs he got,
The feats on pond and river done,
The prodigies of rod and gun;
Till, warming with the tales he told,
Forgotten was the outside cold,
The bitter wind unheeded blew,
From ripening corn the pigeons flew,
The partridge drummed i' the wood, the mink
Went fishing down the river-brink.
In fields with bean or clover gray,
The woodchuck, like a hermit gray,
Peered from the doorway of his cell;
The muskrat plied the mason's trade,
And tier by tier his mud-walls laid;
And from the shagbark overhead
The grizzled squirrel dropped his shell.

Next, the dear aunt, whose smile of cheer
And voice in dreams I see and hear,

The sweetest woman ever Fate
Perverse denied a household mate,
Who, lonely, homeless, not the less
Found peace in love's unselfishness,
And welcome wheresoe'er she went,
A calm and gracious element,
Whose presence seemed the sweet income
And womanly atmosphere of home,
Called up her girlhood memories,
The huskings and the apple-bees,
The sleigh-rides and the summer sails,
Weaving through all the poor details
And homespun warp of circumstance
A golden woof-thread of romance.
For well she kept her genial mood
And simple faith of maidenhood;
Before her still a cloud-land lay,
The mirage loomed across her way;
The morning dew, that dries so soon
With others, glistened at her noon;
Through years of toil and soil and care,
From glossy tress to thin gray hair,
All unprofaned she held apart
The virgin fancies of the heart.
Be shame to him of woman born
Who hath for such but thought of scorn.

There, too, our elder sister plied
Her evening task the stand beside;
A full, rich nature, free to trust,
Truthful and almost sternly just,
Impulsive, earnest, prompt to act,
And make her generous thought a fact,
Keeping with many a light disguise
The secret of self-sacrifice.
O heart sore-tried! thou hast the best
That Heaven itself could give thee, rest,
Rest from all bitter thoughts and things!
How many a poor one's blessing went
With thee beneath the low green tent
Whose curtain never outward swings!

As one who held herself a part
Of all she saw, and let her heart
Against the household bosom lean,
Upon the motley-braided mat
Our youngest and our dearest sat,
Lifting her large, sweet, asking eyes,
Now bathed in the unfading green
And holy peace of Paradise.
Oh, looking from some heavenly hill,
Or from the shade of saintly palms,

Or silver reach of river calms,
Do those large eyes behold me still?
With me one little year ago:
The chill weight of the winter snow
For months upon her grave has lain;
And now, when summer south-winds blow
And brier and harebell bloom again,
I tread the pleasant paths we trod,
I see the violet-sprinkled sod
Whereon she leaned, too frail and weak
The hillside flowers she loved to seek,
Yet following me where'er I went
With dark eyes full of love's content.
The birds are glad; the brier-rose fills
The air with sweetness; all the hills
Stretch green to June's unclouded sky;
But still I wait with ear and eye
For something gone which should be nigh,
A loss in all familiar things,
In flower that blooms, and bird that sings.
And yet, dear heart! remembering thee,
Am I not richer than of old?
Safe in thy immortality,
What change can reach the wealth I hold?
What chance can mar the pearl and gold
Thy love hath left in trust with me?
And while in life's late afternoon,
Where cool and long the shadows grow,
I walk to meet the night that soon
Shall shape and shadow overflow,
I cannot feel that thou art far,
Since near at need the angels are;
And when the sunset gates unbar,
Shall I not see thee waiting stand,
And, white against the evening star,
The welcome of thy beckoning hand?

Brisk wielder of the birch and rule,
The master of the district school
Held at the fire his favored place,
Its warm glow lit a laughing face
Fresh-hued and fair, where scarce appeared
The uncertain prophecy of beard.
He teased the mitten-blinded cat,
Played cross-pins on my uncle's hat,
Sang songs, and told us what befalls
In classic Dartmouth's college halls.
Born the wild Northern hills among,
From whence his yeoman father wrung
By patient toil subsistence scant,
Not competence and yet not want,
He early gained the power to pay

His cheerful, self-reliant way;
Could doff at ease his scholar's gown
To peddle wares from town to town;
Or through the long vacation's reach
In lonely lowland districts teach,
Where all the droll experience found
At stranger hearths in boarding round,
The moonlit skater's keen delight,
The sleigh-drive through the frosty night,
The rustic party, with its rough
Accompaniment of blind-man's-buff,
And whirling-plate, and forfeits paid,
His winter task a pastime made.
Happy the snow-locked homes wherein
He tuned his merry violin,
Or played the athlete in the barn,
Or held the good dame's winding-yarn,
Or mirth-provoking versions told
Of classic legends rare and old,
Wherein the scenes of Greece and Rome
Had all the commonplace of home,
And little seemed at best the odds
'Twixt Yankee pedlers and old gods;
Where Pindus-born Arachthus took
The guise of any grist-mill brook,
And dread Olympus at his will
Became a huckleberry hill.

A careless boy that night he seemed;
But at his desk he had the look
And air of one who wisely schemed,
And hostage from the future took
In trainëd thought and lore of book.
Large-brained, clear-eyed, of such as he
Shall Freedom's young apostles be,
Who, following in War's bloody trail,
Shall every lingering wrong assail;
All chains from limb and spirit strike,
Uplift the black and white alike;
Scatter before their swift advance
The darkness and the ignorance,
The pride, the lust, the squalid sloth,
Which nurtured Treason's monstrous growth,
Made murder pastime, and the hell
Of prison-torture possible;
The cruel lie of caste refute,
Old forms remould, and substitute
For Slavery's lash the freeman's will,
For blind routine, wise-handed skill;
A school-house plant on every hill,
Stretching in radiate nerve-lines thence
The quick wires of intelligence;

Till North and South together brought
Shall own the same electric thought,
In peace a common flag salute,
And, side by side in labor's free
And unresentful rivalry,
Harvest the fields wherein they fought.

Another guest that winter night
Flashed back from lustrous eyes the light.
Unmarked by time, and yet not young,
The honeyed music of her tongue
And words of meekness scarcely told
A nature passionate and bold,
Strong, self-concentred, spurning guide,
Its milder features dwarfed beside
Her unbent will's majestic pride.
She sat among us, at the best,
A not unfeared, half-welcome guest,
Rebuking with her cultured phrase
Our homeliness of words and ways.
A certain pard-like, treacherous grace
Swayed the lithe limbs and drooped the lash,
Lent the white teeth their dazzling flash;
And under low brows, black with night,
Rayed out at times a dangerous light;
The sharp heat-lightnings of her face
Presaging ill to him whom Fate
Condemned to share her love or hate.
A woman tropical, intense
In thought and act, in soul and sense,
She blended in a like degree
The vixen and the devotee,
Revealing with each freak or feint
The temper of Petruchio's Kate,
The raptures of Siena's saint.
Her tapering hand and rounded wrist
Had facile power to form a fist;
The warm, dark languish of her eyes
Was never safe from wrath's surprise.
Brows saintly calm and lips devout
Knew every change of scowl and pout;
And the sweet voice had notes more high
And shrill for social battle-cry.

Since then what old cathedral town
Has missed her pilgrim staff and gown,
What convent-gate has held its lock
Against the challenge of her knock!
Through Smyrna's plague-hushed thoroughfares,
Up sea-set Malta's rocky stairs,
Gray olive slopes of hills that hem
Thy tombs and shrines, Jerusalem,

Or startling on her desert throne
The crazy Queen of Lebanon
With claims fantastic as her own,
Her tireless feet have held their way;
And still, unrestful, bowed, and gray,
She watches under Eastern skies,
With hope each day renewed and fresh,
The Lord's quick coming in the flesh,
Whereof she dreams and prophesies!

Where'er her troubled path may be,
The Lord's sweet pity with her go!
The outward wayward life we see,
The hidden springs we may not know.
Nor is it given us to discern
What threads the fatal sisters spun,
Through what ancestral years has run
The sorrow with the woman born,
What forged her cruel chain of moods,
What set her feet in solitudes,
And held the love within her mute,
What mingled madness in the blood,
A life-long discord and annoy,
Water of tears with oil of joy,
And hid within the folded bud
Perversities of flower and fruit.
It is not ours to separate
The tangled skein of will and fate,
To show what metes and bounds should stand
Upon the soul's debatable land,
And between choice and Providence
Divide the circle of events;
But He who knows our frame is just,
Merciful and compassionate,
And full of sweet assurances
And hope for all the language is,
That He remembereth we are dust!

At last the great logs, crumbling low,
Sent out a dull and duller glow,
The bull's-eye watch that hung in view,
Ticking its weary circuit through,
Pointed with mutely warning sign
Its black hand to the hour of nine.
That sign the pleasant circle broke:
My uncle ceased his pipe to smoke,
Knocked from its bowl the refuse gray,
And laid it tenderly away;
Then roused himself to safely cover
The dull red brands with ashes over.
And while, with care, our mother laid
The work aside, her steps she stayed

One moment, seeking to express
Her grateful sense of happiness
For food and shelter, warmth and health,
And love's contentment more than wealth,
With simple wishes (not the weak,
Vain prayers which no fulfilment seek,
But such as warm the generous heart,
O'er-prompt to do with Heaven its part)
That none might lack, that bitter night,
For bread and clothing, warmth and light.

Within our beds awhile we heard
The wind that round the gables roared,
With now and then a ruder shock,
Which made our very bedsteads rock.
We heard the loosened clapboards tost,
The board-nails snapping in the frost;
And on us, through the unplastered wall,
Felt the light sifted snow-flakes fall.
But sleep stole on, as sleep will do
When hearts are light and life is new;
Faint and more faint the murmurs grew,
Till in the summer-land of dreams
They softened to the sound of streams,
Low stir of leaves, and dip of oars,
And lapsing waves on quiet shores.

Next morn we wakened with the shout
Of merry voices high and clear;
And saw the teamsters drawing near
To break the drifted highways out.
Down the long hillside treading slow
We saw the half-buried oxen go,
Shaking the snow from heads uptost,
Their straining nostrils white with frost.
Before our door the straggling train
Drew up, an added team to gain.
The elders threshed their hands a-cold,
Passed, with the cider-mug, their jokes
From lip to lip; the younger folks
Down the loose snow-banks, wrestling, rolled,
Then toiled again the cavalcade
O'er windy hill, through clogged ravine,
And woodland paths that wound between
Low drooping pine-boughs winter-weighed.
From every barn a team afoot,
At every house a new recruit,
Where, drawn by Nature's subtlest law,
Haply the watchful young men saw
Sweet doorway pictures of the curls
And curious eyes of merry girls,
Lifting their hands in mock defence

Against the snow-ball's compliments,
And reading in each missive tost
The charm with Eden never lost.

We heard once more the sleigh-bells' sound;
And, following where the teamsters led,
The wise old Doctor went his round,
Just pausing at our door to say,
In the brief autocratic way
Of one who, prompt at Duty's call,
Was free to urge her claim on all,
That some poor neighbor sick abed
At night our mother's aid would need.
For, one in generous thought and deed,
What mattered in the sufferer's sight
The Quaker matron's inward light,
The Doctor's mail of Calvin's creed?
All hearts confess the saints elect
Who, twain in faith, in love agree,
And melt not in an acid sect
The Christian pearl of charity!

So days went on: a week had passed
Since the great world was heard from last.
The Almanac we studied o'er,
Read and reread our little store
Of books and pamphlets, scarce a score;
One harmless novel, mostly hid
From younger eyes, a book forbid,
And poetry, (or good or bad,
A single book was all we had,)
Where Ellwood's meek, drab-skirted Muse,
A stranger to the heathen Nine,
Sang, with a somewhat nasal whine,
The wars of David and the Jews.
At last the floundering carrier bore
The village paper to our door.
Lo! broadening outward as we read,
To warmer zones the horizon spread
In panoramic length unrolled
We saw the marvels that it told.
Before us passed the painted Creeks,
And daft McGregor on his raids
In Costa Rica's everglades.
And up Taygetos winding slow
Rode Ypsilanti's Mainote Greeks,
A Turk's head at each saddle-bow!
Welcome to us its week-old news,
Its corner for the rustic Muse,
Its monthly gauge of snow and rain,
Its record, mingling in a breath
The wedding bell and dirge of death:

Jest, anecdote, and love-lorn tale,
The latest culprit sent to jail;
Its hue and cry of stolen and lost,
Its vendue sales and goods at cost,
And traffic calling loud for gain.
We felt the stir of hall and street,
The pulse of life that round us beat;
The chill embargo of the snow
Was melted in the genial glow;
Wide swung again our ice-locked door,
And all the world was ours once more!

Clasp, Angel of the backword look
And folded wings of ashen gray
And voice of echoes far away,
The brazen covers of thy book;
The weird palimpsest old and vast,
Wherein thou hid'st the spectral past;
Where, closely mingling, pale and glow
The characters of joy and woe;
The monographs of outlived years,
Or smile-illumed or dim with tears,
Green hills of life that slope to death,
And haunts of home, whose vistaed trees
Shade off to mournful cypresses
With the white amaranths underneath.
Even while I look, I can but heed
The restless sands' incessant fall,
Importunate hours that hours succeed,
Each clamorous with its own sharp need,
And duty keeping pace with all.
Shut down and clasp with heavy lids;
I hear again the voice that bids
The dreamer leave his dream midway
For larger hopes and graver fears:
Life greatens in these later years,
The century's aloe flowers to-day!

Yet, haply, in some lull of life,
Some Trucc of God which breaks Its strife,
The worldling's eyes shall gather dew,
Dreaming in throngful city ways
Of winter joys his boyhood knew;
And dear and early friends—the few
Who yet remain—shall pause to view
These Flemish pictures of old days;
Sit with me by the homestead hearth,
And stretch the hands of memory forth
To warm them at the wood-fire's blaze!
And thanks untraced to lips unknown
Shall greet me like the odors blown
From unseen meadows newly mown,

Or lilies floating in some pond,
Wood-fringed, the wayside gaze beyond;
The traveller owns the grateful sense
Of sweetness near, he knows not whence,
And, pausing, takes with forehead bare
The benediction of the air.

How Like A Winter Hath My Absence Been - Sonnet 97 By William Shakespeare

How like a winter hath my absence been
From thee, the pleasure of the fleeting year!
What freezings have I felt, what dark days seen!
What old December's bareness every where!
And yet this time remov'd was summer's time;
The teeming autumn, big with rich increase,
Bearing the wanton burden of the prime,
Like widow'd wombs after their lords' decease:
Yet this abundant issue seem'd to me
But hope of orphans and unfather'd fruit;
For summer and his pleasures wait on thee,
And, thou away, the very birds are mute:
Or, if they sing, 'tis with so dull a cheer,
That leaves look pale, dreading the winter's near.

December by John Payne

The roofs are dreary with the drifted rime
And in the air a stillness as of death
Th'approach of some portentousness foresaith.
December comes, the tyrant of the time,
Vaunt-courier of the cold hybernal clime.
Mute is the world for misery; no breath
Nor stir of sound there is, that welcometh
The coming of the Winter's woeful prime.
'Alack! Was ever such a thing as Spring?'
We say, hand-holding to the hearths of Yule.
'Did ever roses blow or throstles sing?'
And in our ears the wild blast shrilleth, 'Fool,
That, in this world of ruin and decay,
Thy heart's hopes buildest on the Summer day!'

Lines Written Among The Euganean Hills by Percy Bysshe Shelley

Many a green isle needs must be
In the deep wide sea of Misery,
Or the mariner, worn and wan,
Never thus could voyage on
Day and night, and night and day,
Drifting on his dreary way,
With the solid darkness black
Closing round his vessel's track;

Whilst above, the sunless sky,
Big with clouds, hangs heavily,
And behind, the tempest fleet
Hurries on with lightning feet,
Riving sail, and cord, and plank,
Till the ship has almost drank
Death from the o'er-brimming deep;
And sinks down, down, like that sleep
When the dreamer seems to be
Weltering through eternity;
And the dim low line before
Of a dark and distant shore
Still recedes, as ever still
Longing with divided will,
But no power to seek or shun,
He is ever drifted on
O'er the unreposing wave
To the haven of the grave.
What, if there no friends will greet;
What, if there no heart will meet
His with love's impatient beat;
Wander wheresoe'er he may,
Can he dream before that day
To find refuge from distress
In friendship's smile, in love's caress?
Then 'twill wreak him little woe
Whether such there be or no:
Senseless is the breast and cold
Which relenting love would fold;
Bloodless are the veins and chill
Which the pulse of pain did fill;
Every little living nerve
That from bitter words did swerve
Round the tortur'd lips and brow,
Are like sapless leaflets now
Frozen upon December's bough.

On the beach of a northern sea
Which tempests shake eternally,
As once the wretch there lay to sleep,
Lies a solitary heap,
One white skull and seven dry bones,
On the margin of the stones,
Where a few gray rushes stand,
Boundaries of the sea and land:
Nor is heard one voice of wail
But the sea-mews, as they sail
O'er the billows of the gale;
Or the whirlwind up and down
Howling, like a slaughter'd town,
When a king in glory rides
Through the pomp of fratricides:

Those unburied bones around
There is many a mournful sound;
There is no lament for him,
Like a sunless vapour, dim,
Who once cloth'd with life and thought
What now moves nor murmurs not.

Ay, many flowering islands lie
In the waters of wide Agony:
To such a one this morn was led
My bark, by soft winds piloted:
'Mid the mountains Euganean
I stood listening to the paean
With which the legion'd rooks did hail
The sun's uprise majestical;
Gathering round with wings all hoar,
Through the dewy mist they soar
Like gray shades, till the eastern heaven
Bursts, and then, as clouds of even,
Fleck'd with fire and azure, lie
In the unfathomable sky,
So their plumes of purple grain,
Starr'd with drops of golden rain,
Gleam above the sunlight woods,
As in silent multitudes
On the morning's fitful gale
Through the broken mist they sail,
And the vapours cloven and gleaming
Follow, down the dark steep streaming,
Till all is bright, and clear, and still,
Round the solitary hill.

Beneath is spread like a green sea
The waveless plain of Lombardy,
Bounded by the vaporous air,
Islanded by cities fair;
Underneath Day's azure eyes
Ocean's nursling, Venice lies,
A peopled labyrinth of walls,
Amphitrite's destin'd halls,
Which her hoary sire now paves
With his blue and beaming waves.
Lo! the sun upsprings behind,
Broad, red, radiant, half-reclin'd
On the level quivering line
Of the water crystalline;
And before that chasm of light,
As within a furnace bright,
Column, tower, and dome, and spire,
Shine like obelisks of fire,
Pointing with inconstant motion
From the altar of dark ocean

To the sapphire-tinted skies;
As the flames of sacrifice
From the marble shrines did rise,
As to pierce the dome of gold
Where Apollo spoke of old.

Sun-girt City, thou hast been
Ocean's child, and then his queen;
Now is come a darker day,
And thou soon must be his prey,
If the power that rais'd thee here
Hallow so thy watery bier.
A less drear ruin then than now,
With thy conquest-branded brow
Stooping to the slave of slaves
From thy throne, among the waves
Wilt thou be, when the sea-mew
Flies, as once before it flew,
O'er thine isles depopulate,
And all is in its ancient state,
Save where many a palace gate
With green sea-flowers overgrown
Like a rock of Ocean's own,
Topples o'er the abandon'd sea
As the tides change sullenly.
The fisher on his watery way,
Wandering at the close of day,
Will spread his sail and seize his oar
Till he pass the gloomy shore,
Lest thy dead should, from their sleep
Bursting o'er the starlight deep,
Lead a rapid masque of death
O'er the waters of his path.
Those who alone thy towers behold
Quivering through a{:e}real gold,
As I now behold them here,
Would imagine not they were
Sepulchres, where human forms,
Like pollution-nourish'd worms,
To the corpse of greatness cling,
Murder'd, and now mouldering:
But if Freedom should awake
In her omnipotence, and shake
From the Celtic Anarch's hold
All the keys of dungeons cold,
Where a hundred cities lie
Chain'd like thee, ingloriously,
Thou and all thy sister band
Might adorn this sunny land,
Twining memories of old time
With new virtues more sublime;
If not, perish thou and they,

Clouds which stain truth's rising day
By her sun consum'd away—
Earth can spare ye! while like flowers,
In the waste of years and hours,
From your dust new nations spring
With more kindly blossoming.

Perish—let there only be
Floating o'er thy hearthless sea
As the garment of thy sky
Clothes the world immortally,
One remembrance, more sublime
Than the tatter'd pall of time,
Which scarce hides thy visage wan:
That a tempest-cleaving Swan
Of the sons of Albion,
Driven from his ancestral streams
By the might of evil dreams,
Found a nest in thee; and Ocean
Welcom'd him with such emotion
That its joy grew his, and sprung
From his lips like music flung
O'er a mighty thunder-fit,
Chastening terror: what though yet
Poesy's unfailing river,
Which through Albion winds forever
Lashing with melodious wave
Many a sacred Poet's grave,
Mourn its latest nursling fled!
What though thou with all thy dead
Scarce can for this fame repay
Aught thine own, oh, rather say
Though thy sins and slaveries foul
Overcloud a sunlike soul!
As the ghost of Homer clings
Round Scamander's wasting springs;
As divinest Shakespeare's might
Fills Avon and the world with light
Like omniscient power which he
Imag'd 'mid mortality;
As the love from Petrarch's urn
Yet amid yon hills doth burn,
A quenchless lamp by which the heart
Sees things unearthly; so thou art,
Mighty spirit: so shall be
The City that did refuge thee.

Lo, the sun floats up the sky
Like thought-winged Liberty,
Till the universal light
Seems to level plain and height;
From the sea a mist has spread,

And the beams of morn lie dead
On the towers of Venice now,
Like its glory long ago.
By the skirts of that gray cloud
Many-domed Padua proud
Stands, a peopled solitude,
'Mid the harvest-shining plain,
Where the peasant heaps his grain
In the garner of his foe,
And the milk-white oxen slow
With the purple vintage strain,
Heap'd upon the creaking wain,
That the brutal Celt may swill
Drunken sleep with savage will;
And the sickle to the sword
Lies unchang'd though many a lord,
Like a weed whose shade is poison,
Overgrows this region's foison,
Sheaves of whom are ripe to come
To destruction's harvest-home:
Men must reap the things they sow,
Force from force must ever flow,
Or worse; but 'tis a bitter woe
That love or reason cannot change
The despot's rage, the slave's revenge.

Padua, thou within whose walls
Those mute guests at festivals,
Son and Mother, Death and Sin,
Play'd at dice for Ezzelin,
Till Death cried, 'I win, I win!'
And Sin curs'd to lose the wager,
But Death promis'd, to assuage her,
That he would petition for
Her to be made Vice-Emperor,
When the destin'd years were o'er,
Over all between the Po
And the eastern Alpine snow,
Under the mighty Austrian.
Sin smil'd so as Sin only can,
And since that time, ay, long before,
Both have rul'd from shore to shore,
That incestuous pair, who follow
Tyrants as the sun the swallow,
As Repentance follows Crime,
And as changes follow Time.

In thine halls the lamp of learning,
Padua, now no more is burning;
Like a meteor, whose wild way
Is lost over the grave of day,
It gleams betray'd and to betray:

Once remotest nations came
To adore that sacred flame,
When it lit not many a hearth
On this cold and gloomy earth:
Now new fires from antique light
Spring beneath the wide world's might;
But their spark lies dead in thee,
Trampled out by Tyranny.
As the Norway woodman quells,
In the depth of piny dells,
One light flame among the brakes,
While the boundless forest shakes,
And its mighty trunks are torn
By the fire thus lowly born:
The spark beneath his feet is dead,
He starts to see the flames it fed
Howling through the darken'd sky
With myriad tongues victoriously,
And sinks down in fear: so thou,
O Tyranny, beholdest now
Light around thee, and thou hearest
The loud flames ascend, and fearest:
Grovel on the earth; ay, hide
In the dust thy purple pride!

Noon descends around me now:
'Tis the noon of autumn's glow,
When a soft and purple mist
Like a vaporous amethyst,
Or an air-dissolved star
Mingling light and fragrance, far
From the curv'd horizon's bound
To the point of Heaven's profound,
Fills the overflowing sky;
And the plains that silent lie
Underneath, the leaves unsodden
Where the infant Frost has trodden
With his morning-winged feet,
Whose bright print is gleaming yet;
And the red and golden vines,
Piercing with their trellis'd lines
The rough, dark-skirted wilderness;
The dun and bladed grass no less,
Pointing from his hoary tower
In the windless air; the flower
Glimmering at my feet; the line
Of the olive-sandall'd Apennine
In the south dimly islanded;
And the Alps, whose snows are spread
High between the clouds and sun;
And of living things each one;
And my spirit which so long

Darken'd this swift stream of song,
Interpenetrated lie
By the glory of the sky:
Be it love, light, harmony,
Odour, or the soul of all
Which from Heaven like dew doth fall,
Or the mind which feeds this verse
Peopling the lone universe.

Noon descends, and after noon
Autumn's evening meets me soon,
Leading the infantine moon,
And that one star, which to her
Almost seems to minister
Half the crimson light she brings
From the sunset's radiant springs:
And the soft dreams of the morn
(Which like winged winds had borne
To that silent isle, which lies
Mid remember'd agonies,
The frail bark of this lone being)
Pass, to other sufferers fleeing,
And its ancient pilot, Pain,
Sits beside the helm again.

Other flowering isles must be
In the sea of Life and Agony:
Other spirits float and flee
O'er that gulf: even now, perhaps,
On some rock the wild wave wraps,
With folded wings they waiting sit
For my bark, to pilot it
To some calm and blooming cove,
Where for me, and those I love,
May a windless bower be built,
Far from passion, pain and guilt,
In a dell mid lawny hills,
Which the wild sea-murmur fills,
And soft sunshine, and the sound
Of old forests echoing round,
And the light and smell divine
Of all flowers that breathe and shine:
We may live so happy there,
That the Spirits of the Air,
Envying us, may even entice
To our healing paradise
The polluting multitude;
But their rage would be subdu'd
By that clime divine and calm,
And the winds whose wings rain balm
On the uplifted soul, and leaves
Under which the bright sea heaves;

While each breathless interval
In their whisperings musical
The inspired soul supplies
With its own deep melodies,
And the love which heals all strife
Circling, like the breath of life,
All things in that sweet abode
With its own mild brotherhood:
They, not it, would change; and soon
Every sprite beneath the moon
Would repent its envy vain,
And the earth grow young again.

Sicily December 1908 by Henry Van Dyke

O garden isle, beloved by Sun and Sea,
Whose bluest billows kiss thy curving bays,
Whose light infolds thy hills with golden rays,
Filling with fruit each dark-leaved orange-tree,
What hidden hatred hath the Earth for thee,
That once again, in these dark, dreadful days,
Breaks forth in trembling rage, and swiftly lays
Thy beauty waste in wreck and agony!
Is Nature, then, a strife of jealous powers,
And man the plaything of unconscious fate?
Not so, my troubled heart! God reigns above,
And man is greatest in his darkest hours.
Walking amid the cities desolate,
Behold the Son of God in human love!

December by John Bannister Tabb

Dull sky above, dead leaves below;
And hungry winds that whining go.
Like faithful hounds upon the track
Of one beloved that comes not back.

December Sales Drive by Daniel Sheehan

December Sales Drive by Daniel Sheehan
Could Christmas really come
Not with adverts on the telly
But in good grace with charity
For those with less or none at all
Or is Jesus just a corporation -
A sales drive for December?

The Idlers Calendar. Twelve Sonnets For The Year - December by Wilfred Scawen Blunt

AWAY TO EGYPT

Enough, enough! This winter is too rude,

Too dark of countenance, of tooth too keen.
Nature finds rebels now in flesh and blood,
And hearts grow sick for change and eyes for green.
Let us away! What profits it that men
Are wise as gods, if winter holds its sway,
If blood be chilled, and numbness clasp the brain?
Frost is too stubborn. Let us then away!

Away to Egypt! There we may forget
All but the presence of the blessed sun.
There in our tents well--housed, sublimely set
Under a pyramid, with horse and gun,
We may make terms with Nature and, awhile,
Put as it were our souls to grass, and run
Barefooted and barehearted in the smile
Of that long summer which still girds the Nile.

The December Rose By Edith Nesbit
Here's a rose that blows for Chloe,
Fair as ever a rose in June was,
Now the garden's silent, snowy,
Where the burning summer noon was.

In your garden's summer glory
One poor corner, shelved and shady,
Told no rosy, radiant story,
Grew no rose to grace its lady.

What shuts sun out shuts out snow too;
From his nook your secret lover
Shows what slighted roses grow to
When the rose you chose is over.

On The Death Of Major Whitefoord, December 15th 1825 by Eliza Acton
Like blighted leaves, around us fall
The young, the gifted, and the brave;
And still the most belov'd of all
Seem earliest fated to the grave.

With health the morning saw thee blest,
And gladness brighten'd o'er thy brow;
When ev'ning flung across the West
Her dark'ning shadows,-where wert thou?

Cold, cold for ever was thy heart,
And hush'd its pulse of joy, or pain:
Life's silver cord was torn apart,
The golden bowl was broken then.

Without one sign of warning giv'n,

To tell of danger lurking near,
With sudden wrench the chain was riv'n,
Which kept thy pilgrim footsteps here.

Yes! ere the sun whose dawning ray
Upon thy peaceful waking shone,
Withdrew from heav'n the light of day,
Thy spirit to its rest was gone.

And many a mourner o'er thy bed,
In pale, and speechless anguish hung;
And burning tears above thee shed,
From agony's deep source were wrung.

Ev'n strangers wept for thee !-and yet,
By voices to thine ear unknown,
With fulness of unfeign'd regret,
Thy name is breath'd in sorrow's tone.

And, oh! through long, long years to come,
Shall sad, but tend'rest thoughts of thee,
Within the circle of thy home,
Be shrin'd and cherish'd faithfully!

December Matins by Alfred Austin
` Why, on this drear December morn,
Dost thou, lone Misselthrush, rehearse thy chanting?
The corals have been rifled from the thorn,
The pastures lie undenizened and lorn,
And everywhere around there seems a something wanting.''
Whereat, as tho' awondering at my wonder,
And brooded somewhere nigh a love-mate nesting,
He more loud and longer still
'Gan to tremble and to trill,
Height after height of sound robustly breasting;
As if o'erhead were Heaven of blue, and under,
Fresh green leafage, and he would
Cleave with shafts of hardihood
The mists asunder.

Only the singer it is foresees,
Only the Poet has the voice foretelling.
When the ways harden and the sedge-pools freeze,
He hears light-hearted Spring upon the breeze,
And feels the hawthorn buds mysteriously swelling.
Though to the eaves the icicles are clinging,
Or from the sunward gables dripping, dripping,
He with inward gaze beholds
Liberated flocks and folds,
The runnels leaping, and the young lambs skipping,
And dauntless daffodils anew upspringing,

So throughout the wintry days
Meditates prophetic lays,
And keeps on singing.

Not the full-volumed Springtime song,
Not April's note with rapture overflowing,
Melodious cadence, early, late, and long,
Now low and suing, now serenely strong,
But the heart's intimations musically showing
That Love and Verse are never out of season.
Though the winds bluster, and the branches splinter,
He, through cold and dire distress,
Companioned by cheerfulness,
Descries young Mayday through the mask of Winter.
Doubt and despair to him were veilèd treason,
Fashioned never to despond,
By Foreseeing far beyond
The range of Reason.

Therefore, brave bird, sing on, for some to hear
If faintly, fitfully, and though to-morrow
Will be the shortest day of all the year,
Though fields be flowerless and fallows drear,
And earth seems cherishing some secret sorrow,
The dawn will come when it anew will glisten
With tears of gladness, glen and dingle waken,
Winter's tents be furled and routed,
April notes be sung and shouted,
Over the fleeing host and camp forsaken;
The nightingale ne'er cease, the cuckoo christen
Hedgerow posies with its call,
And unto glee and madrigal
The whole world listen.

To A Lady Who Presented to The Author A Lock Of Hair Braided With His
Own And Appointed A Night In December To Meet Him In The Garden by
Lord Byron
These locks, which fondly thus entwine,
In firmer chains our hearts confine
Than all th' unmeaning protestations
Which swell with nonsense love orations.
Our love is fix'd, I think we've proved it,
Nor time, nor place, nor art have moved it;
Then wherefore should we sigh and whine,
With groundless jealousy repine,
With silly whims and fancies frantic,
Merely to make our love romantic?
Why should you weep like Lydia Languish,
And fret with self-created anguish?
Or doom the lover you have chosen,
On winter to nights to sigh half frozen;

In leafless shades to sue for pardon,
Only because the scene's a garden?
For gardens seem, by one consent
(Since Shakespeare set the precedent,
Since Juliet first declared her passion),
To from the place of assignation.
Oh! would some modern muse inspire,
And seat her by a sea-coal fire;
Or had the bard at Christmas written,
And laid the scene of love in Britain,
He surely, in commiseration,
Had changed the place of declaration.
In Italy I've no objection,
Warm nights are proper for reflection;
But here our climate is so rigid,
That love itself is rather frigid:
Think on our chilly situation,
And curb this rage for imitation.
Then let us meet, as oft we've done,
Beneath the influence of the sun;
Or, if at midnight I must meet you,
Within your mansion let me greet you:
There we can love for hours together,
Much better, in such snowy weather,
Than placed in all th' Arcadian groves
That ever witness'd rural loves;
Then, if my passion fail to please,
Next night I'll be content to freeze;
No more I'll give a loose to laughter,
But curse my fate for ever after.

Winter Stores by Charlotte Bronte
We take from life one little share,
And say that this shall be
A space, redeemed from toil and care,
From tears and sadness free.

And, haply, Death unstrings his bow,
And Sorrow stands apart,
And, for a little while, we know
The sunshine of the heart.

Existence seems a summer eve,
Warm, soft, and full of peace,
Our free, unfettered feelings give
The soul its full release.

A moment, then, it takes the power
To call up thoughts that throw
Around that charmed and hallowed hour,
This life's divinest glow.

But Time, though viewlessly it flies,
And slowly, will not stay;
Alike, through clear and clouded skies,
It cleaves its silent way.

Alike the bitter cup of grief,
Alike the draught of bliss,
Its progress leaves but moment brief
For baffled lips to kiss

The sparkling draught is dried away,
The hour of rest is gone,
And urgent voices, round us, say,
"'Ho, lingerer, hasten on!"

And has the soul, then, only gained,
From this brief time of ease,
A moment's rest, when overstrained,
One hurried glimpse of peace?

No; while the sun shone kindly o'er us,
And flowers bloomed round our feet,
While many a bud of joy before us
Unclosed its petals sweet,

An unseen work within was plying;
Like honey-seeking bee,
From flower to flower, unwearied, flying,
Laboured one faculty,

Thoughtful for Winter's future sorrow,
Its gloom and scarcity;
Prescient to-day, of want to-morrow,
Toiled quiet Memory.

'Tis she that from each transient pleasure
Extracts a lasting good;
'Tis she that finds, in summer, treasure
To serve for winter's food.

And when Youth's summer day is vanished,
And Age brings Winter's stress,
Her stores, with hoarded sweets replenished,
Life's evening hours will bless.

In Drear Nighted December by John Keats
In drear-nighted December,
Too happy, happy tree,
Thy branches ne'er remember
Their green felicity:

The north cannot undo them
With a sleety whistle through them;
Nor frozen thawings glue them
From budding at the prime.

In drear-nighted December,
Too happy, happy brook,
Thy bubblings ne'er remember
Apollo's summer look;
But with a sweet forgetting,
They stay their crystal fretting,
Never, never petting
About the frozen time.

Ah! would 'twere so with many
A gentle girl and boy!
But were there ever any
Writhed not at passed joy?
The feel of not to feel it,
When there is none to heal it
Nor numbed sense to steel it,
Was never said in rhyme.

The Foolish Fir Tree by Henry Van Dyke
A tale that the poet Rückert told
To German children, in days of old;
Disguised in a random, rollicking rhyme
Like a merry mummer of ancient time,
And sent, in its English dress, to please
The little folk of the Christmas trees.

A little fir grew in the midst of the wood
Contented and happy, as young trees should.
His body was straight and his boughs were clean;
And summer and winter the bountiful sheen
Of his needles bedecked him, from top to root,
In a beautiful, all-the-year, evergreen suit.

But a trouble came into his heart one day,
When he saw that the other trees were gay
In the wonderful raiment that summer weaves
Of manifold shapes and kinds of leaves:
He looked at his needles so stiff and small,
And thought that his dress was the poorest of all.
Then jealousy clouded the little tree's mind,
And he said to himself, "It was not very kind
"To give such an ugly old dress to a tree!
"If the fays of the forest would only ask me,
"I'd tell them how I should like to be dressed,
"In a garment of gold, to bedazzle the rest!"
So he fell asleep, but his dreams were bad.

When he woke in the morning, his heart was glad;
For every leaf that his boughs could hold
Was made of the brightest beaten gold.
I tell you, children, the tree was proud;
He was something above the common crowd;
And he tinkled his leaves, as if he would say
To a pedlar who happened to pass that way,
"Just look at me! don't you think I am fine?
"And wouldn't you like such a dress as mine?"
"Oh, yes!" said the man, "and I really guess
I must fill my pack with your beautiful dress."
So he picked the golden leaves with care,
And left the little tree shivering there.

"Oh, why did I wish for golden leaves?"
The fir-tree said, "I forgot that thieves
"Would be sure to rob me in passing by.
"If the fairies would give me another try,
"I'd wish for something that cost much less,
"And be satisfied with glass for my dress!"
Then he fell asleep; and, just as before,
The fairies granted his wish once more.
When the night was gone, and the sun rose clear,
The tree was a crystal chandelier;
And it seemed, as he stood in the morning light,
That his branches were covered with jewels bright.
"Aha!" said the tree. "This is something great!"
And he held himself up, very proud and straight;
But a rude young wind through the forest dashed,
In a reckless temper, and quickly smashed
The delicate leaves. With a clashing sound
They broke into pieces and fell on the ground,
Like a silvery, shimmering shower of hail,
And the tree stood naked and bare to the gale.

Then his heart was sad; and he cried, "Alas
"For my beautiful leaves of shining glass!
"Perhaps I have made another mistake
"In choosing a dress so easy to break.
"If the fairies only would hear me again
"I'd ask them for something both pretty and plain:
"It wouldn't cost much to grant my request,
"In leaves of green lettuce I'd like to be dressed!"
By this time the fairies were laughing, I know;
But they gave him his wish in a second; and so
With leaves of green lettuce, all tender and sweet,
The tree was arrayed, from his head to his feet.
"I knew it!" he cried, "I was sure I could find
"The sort of a suit that would be to my mind.
"There's none of the trees has a prettier dress,
"And none as attractive as I am, I guess."
But a goat, who was taking an afternoon walk,

By chance overheard the fir-tree's talk.
So he came up close for a nearer view;
"My salad!" he bleated, "I think so too!
"You're the most attractive kind of a tree,
"And I want your leaves for my five-o'clock tea."
So he ate them all without saying grace,
And walked away with a grin on his face;
While the little tree stood in the twilight dim,
With never a leaf on a single limb.

Then he sighed and groaned; but his voice was weak
He was so ashamed that he could not speak.
He knew at last that he had been a fool,
To think of breaking the forest rule,
And choosing a dress himself to please,
Because he envied the other trees.
But it couldn't be helped, it was now too late,
He must make up his mind to a leafless fate!
So he let himself sink in a slumber deep,
But he moaned and he tossed in his troubled sleep,
Till the morning touched him with joyful beam,
And he woke to find it was all a dream.
For there in his evergreen dress he stood,
A pointed fir in the midst of the wood!
His branches were sweet with the balsam smell,
His needles were green when the white snow fell.
And always contented and happy was he,—
The very best kind of a Christmas tree.

The Death Of The Old Year by Alfred Lord Tennyson
Full knee-deep lies the winter snow,
And the winter winds are wearily sighing:
Toll ye the church bell sad and slow,
And tread softly and speak low,
For the old year lies a-dying.
Old year you must not die;
You came to us so readily,
You lived with us so steadily,
Old year you shall not die.

He lieth still: he doth not move:
He will not see the dawn of day.
He hath no other life above.
He gave me a friend and a true truelove
And the New-year will take 'em away.
Old year you must not go;
So long you have been with us,
Such joy as you have seen with us,
Old year, you shall not go.

He froth'd his bumpers to the brim;

A jollier year we shall not see.
But tho' his eyes are waxing dim,
And tho' his foes speak ill of him,
He was a friend to me.
Old year, you shall not die;
We did so laugh and cry with you,
I've half a mind to die with you,
Old year, if you must die.

He was full of joke and jest,
But all his merry quips are o'er.
To see him die across the waste
His son and heir doth ride post-haste,
But he'll be dead before.
Every one for his own.
The night is starry and cold, my friend,
And the New-year blithe and bold, my friend,
Comes up to take his own.

How hard he breathes! over the snow
I heard just now the crowing cock.
The shadows flicker to and fro:
The cricket chirps: the light burns low:
'Tis nearly twelve o'clock.
Shake hands, before you die.
Old year, we'll dearly rue for you:
What is it we can do for you?
Speak out before you die.

His face is growing sharp and thin.
Alack! our friend is gone,
Close up his eyes: tie up his chin:
Step from the corpse, and let him in
That standeth there alone,
And waiteth at the door.
There's a new foot on the floor, my friend,
And a new face at the door, my friend,
A new face at the door.

Christmas At Sea by Robert Louis Stevenson

The sheets were frozen hard, and they cut the naked hand;
The decks were like a slide, where a seaman scarce could stand;
The wind was a nor'-wester, blowing squally off the sea;
And cliffs and spouting breakers were the only things a-lee.
They heard the suff a-roaring before the break of day;
But 'twas only with the peep of light we saw how ill we lay.
We tumbled every hand on deck instanter, with a shout,
And we gave her the maintops'l, and stood by to go about.

All day we tacked and tacked between the South Head and the North;
All day we hauled the frozen sheets, and got no further forth;

All day as cold as charity, in bitter pain and dread,
For very life and nature we tacked from head to head.

We gave the South a wider berth, for there the tide-race roared;
But every tack we made we brought the North Head close aboard.
So's we saw the cliff and houses and the breakers running high,
And the coastguard in his garden, with his glass against his eye.

The frost was on the village roofs as white as ocean foam;
The good red fires were burning bright in every longshore home;
The windows sparkled clear, and the chimneys volleyed out;
And I vow we sniffed the victuals as the vessel went about.

The bells upon the church were rung with a mighty jovial cheer;
For it's just that I should tell you how (of all days in the year)
This day of our adversity was blessèd Christmas morn,
And the house above the coastguard's was the house where I was born.

O well I saw the pleasant room, the pleasant faces there,
My mother's silver spectacles, my father's silver hair;
And well I saw the firelight, like a flight of homely elves,
Go dancing round the china plates that stand upon the shelves.

And well I knew the talk they had, the talk that was of me,
Of the shadow on the household and the son that went to sea;
And O the wicked fool I seemed, in every kind of way,
To be here and hauling frozen ropes on blessèd Christmas Day.

They lit the high sea-light, and the dark began to fall.
"All hands to loose topgallant sails," I heard the captain call.
"By the Lord, she'll never stand it," our first mate, Jackson, cried.
. . . ."It's the one way or the other, Mr. Jackson," he replied.

She staggered to her bearings, but the sails were new and good,
And the ship smelt up to windward just as though she understood;
As the winter's day was ending, in the entry of the night,
We cleared the weary headland, and passed below the light.

And they heaved a mighty breath, every soul on board but me,
As they saw her nose again pointing handsome out to sea;
But all that I could think of, in the darkness and the cold,
Was just that I was leaving home and my folks were growing old.

December 23rd 1879 by George MacDonald
I.
A thousand houses of poesy stand around me everywhere;
They fill the earth and they fill my thought, they are in and above the
air;
But to-night they have shut their doors, they have shut their shining
windows fair,
And I am left in a desert world, with an aching as if of care.

II.

Cannot I break some little nut and get at the poetry in it?
Cannot I break the shining egg of some all but hatched heavenly linnet?
Cannot I find some beauty-worm, and its moony cocoon-silk spin it?
Cannot I find my all but lost day in the rich content of a minute?

III.

I will sit me down, all aching and tired, in the midst of this
never-unclosing
Of door or window that makes it look as if truth herself were dozing;
I will sit me down and make me a tent, call it poetizing or prosing,
Of what may be lying within my reach, things at my poor disposing!

IV.

Now what is nearest?-My conscious self. Here I sit quiet and say:
'Lo, I myself am already a house of poetry solemn and gay!
But, alas, the windows are shut, all shut: 'tis a cold and foggy day,
And I have not now the light to see what is in me the same alway!'

V.

Nay, rather I'll say: 'I am a nut in the hard and frozen ground;
Above is the damp and frozen air, the cold blue sky all round;
And the power of a leafy and branchy tree is in me crushed and bound
Till the summer come and set it free from the grave-clothes
in which it is wound!'

VI.

But I bethink me of something better!-something better, yea best!
'I am lying a voiceless, featherless thing in God's own perfect nest;
And the voice and the song are growing within me, slowly lifting my
breast;
And his wide night-wings are closed about me, for his sun is down in the
west!'

VII.

Doors and windows, tents and grave-clothes, winters and eggs and seeds,
Ye shall all be opened and broken and torn; ye are but to serve my needs!
On the will of the Father all lovely things are strung like a string of
beads
For his heart to give the obedient child that the will of the father
heeds.

Christmas Bells by Henry Wadsworth Longfellow
I heard the bells on Christmas Day
Their old, familiar carols play,
And wild and sweet
The words repeat
Of peace on earth, good-will to men!

And thought how, as the day had come,

The belfries of all Christendom
Had rolled along
The unbroken song
Of peace on earth, good-will to men!

Till, ringing, singing on its way
The world revolved from night to day,
A voice, a chime,
A chant sublime
Of peace on earth, good-will to men!

Then from each black, accursed mouth
The cannon thundered in the South,
And with the sound
The Carols drowned
Of peace on earth, good-will to men!

And in despair I bowed my head;
'There is no peace on earth,' I said;
'For hate is strong,
And mocks the song
Of peace on earth, good-will to men!'

Then pealed the bells more loud and deep:
'God is not dead; nor doth he sleep!
The Wrong shall fail,
The Right prevail,
With peace on earth, good-will to men!'

Ceremonies For Christmas by Robert Herrick
Come, bring with a noise,
My merry, merry boys,
The Christmas Log to the firing;
While my good Dame, she
Bids ye all be free;
And drink to your heart's desiring.

With the last year's brand
Light the new block, and
For good success in his spending,
On your Psaltries play,
That sweet luck may
Come while the log is a-tinding.

Drink now the strong beer,
Cut the white loaf here,
The while the meat is a-shredding;
For the rare mince-pie
And the plums stand by
To fill the paste that's a-kneading.

Every time would have its song
If the heart were right,
Seeing Love all tender-strong
Fills the day and night.

Weary drop the hands of Prayer
Calling out for peace;
Love always and everywhere
Sings and does not cease.

Fear, the caitiff, through the night
Silent peers about;
Love comes singing with a light
And doth cast him out.

Hate and Guile and Wrath and Doubt
Never try to sing;
If they did, oh, what a rout
Anguished ears would sting!

Pride indeed will sometimes aim
At the finer speech,
But the best that he can frame
Is a peacock-screech.

Greed will also sometimes try:
Happiness he hunts!
But his dwelling is a sty,
And his tones are grunts.

Faith will sometimes raise a song
Soaring up to heaven,
Then she will be silent long,
And will weep at even.

Hope has many a gladsome note
Now and then to pipe;
But, alas, he has the throat
Of a bird unripe.

Often Joy a stave will start
Which the welkin rends,
But it always breaks athwart,
And untimely ends.

Grief, who still for death doth long,
Always self-abhorred,
Has but one low, troubled song,
I am sorry, Lord

But Love singeth in the vault.
Singeth on the stair;
Even for Sorrow will not halt,
Singeth everywhere.

For the great Love everywhere
Over all doth glow;
Draws his birds up trough the air,
Tends his birds below.

And with songs ascending sheer
Love-born Love replies,
Singing Father in his ear
Where she bleeding lies.

Therefore, if my heart were right
I should sing out clear,
Sing aloud both day and night
Every month in the year!

At The Entering Of The New Year by Thomas Hardy
I
(OLD STYLE)
Our songs went up and out the chimney,
And roused the home-gone husbandmen;
Our allemands, our heys, poussettings,
Our hands-across and back again,
Sent rhythmic throbbings through the casements
On to the white highway,
Where nighted farers paused and muttered,
"Keep it up well, do they!"

The contrabasso's measured booming
Sped at each bar to the parish bounds,
To shepherds at their midnight lambings,
To stealthy poachers on their rounds;
And everybody caught full duly
The notes of our delight,
As Time unrobed the Youth of Promise
Hailed by our sanguine sight.

II
(NEW STYLE)
We stand in the dusk of a pine-tree limb,
As if to give ear to the muffled peal,
Brought or withheld at the breeze's whim;
But our truest heed is to words that steal
From the mantled ghost that looms in the gray,
And seems, so far as our sense can see,
To feature bereaved Humanity,
As it sighs to the imminent year its say:

"O stay without, O stay without,
Calm comely Youth, untasked, untired;
Though stars irradiate thee about
Thy entrance here is undesired.
Open the gate not, mystic one;
Must we avow what we would close confine?
With thee, good friend, we would have converse none,
Albeit the fault may not be thine."

Ring Out, Wild Bells - Christmas Poem by Alfred, Lord Tennyson
Ring out, wild bells, to the wild sky,
The flying cloud, the frosty light;
The year is dying in the night;
Ring out, wild bells, and let him die.

Ring out the old, ring in the new,
Ring, happy bells, across the snow:
The year is going, let him go;
Ring out the false, ring in the true.

Ring out the grief that saps the mind,
For those that here we see no more,
Ring out the feud of rich and poor,
Ring in redress to all mankind.

Ring out a slowly dying cause,
And ancient forms of party strife;
Ring in the nobler modes of life,
With sweeter manners, purer laws.

Ring out the want, the care the sin,
The faithless coldness of the times;
Ring out, ring out my mournful rhymes,
But ring the fuller minstrel in.

Ring out false pride in place and blood,
The civic slander and the spite;
Ring In the love of truth and right,
Ring in the common love of good.

Ring out old shapes of foul disease,
Ring out the narrowing lust of gold;
Ring out the thousand wars of old,
Ring in the thousand years of peace.

Ring in the valiant man and free,
The larger heart, the kindlier hand;
Ring out the darkness of the land,
Ring in the Christ that is to be.

December by John Clare

While snow the window-panes bedim,
The fire curls up a sunny charm,
Where, creaming o'er the pitcher's rim,
The flowering ale is set to warm;
Mirth, full of joy as summer bees,
Sits there, its pleasures to impart,
And children, 'tween their parent's knees,
Sing scraps of carols o'er by heart.

And some, to view the winter weathers,
Climb up the window-seat with glee,
Likening the snow to falling feathers,
In fancy infant ecstasy;
Laughing, with superstitious love,
O'er visions wild that youth supplies,
Of people pulling geese above,
And keeping Christmas in the skies.

As tho' the homestead trees were drest,
In lieu of snow, with dancing leaves,
As tho' the sun-dried martin's nest,
Instead of ickles, hung the eaves,
The children hail the happy day
As if the snow were April's grass,
And pleas'd, as 'neath the warmth of May,
Sport o'er the water froze as glass.

The Twenty Second Of December by William Cullen Bryant

Wild was the day; the wintry sea
Moaned sadly on New-England's strand,
When first the thoughtful and the free,
Our fathers, trod the desert land.

They little thought how pure a light,
With years, should gather round that day;
How love should keep their memories bright,
How wide a realm their sons should sway.

Green are their bays; but greener still
Shall round their spreading fame be wreathed,
And regions, now untrod, shall thrill
With reverence when their names are breathed.

Till where the sun, with softer fires,
Looks on the vast Pacific's sleep,
The children of the pilgrim sires
This hallowed day like us shall keep.

The Shepheardes Calender: December by Edmund Spenser

He gentle shepheard satte beside a springe,
All in the shadowe of a bushy brere,
That Colin hight, which wel could pype and singe,
For he of Tityrus his songs did lere.
There as he satte in secreate shade alone,
Thus gan he make of loue his piteous mone.
O soueraigne Pan thou God of shepheards all,
Which of our tender Lambkins takest keepe:
And when our flocks into mischaunce mought fall,
Doest save from mischeife the vnwary sheepe:
Als of their maisters hast no lesse regarde,
Then of the flocks, which thou doest watch and ward:

I thee beseche (so be thou deigne to heare,
Rude ditties tund to shepheards Oaten reede,
Or if I euer sonet song so cleare,
As it with pleasaunce mought thy fancie feede)
Hearken awhile from thy greene cabinet,
The rurall song of carefull Colinet.

Whilome in youth, when flowrd my ioyfull spring,
Like Swallow swift I wandred here and there:
For heate of heedlesse lust me so did sting,
That I of doubted daunger had no feare.
I went the wastefull woodes and forest wyde,
Withouten dreade of Wolues to bene espyed.

I wont to raunge amydde the mazie thickette,
And gather nuttes to make me Christmas game:
And ioyed oft to chace the trembling Pricket,
Or hunt the hartlesse hare, til shee were tame.
What wreaked I of wintrye ages waste,
Tho deemed I, my spring would euer laste.

How often haue I scaled the craggie Oke,
All to dislodge the Rauen of her neste:
Howe haue I wearied with many a stroke,
The stately Walnut tree, the while the rest
Vnder the tree fell all for nuts at strife:
For ylike to me was libertee and lyfe.

And for I was in thilke same looser yeares,
(Whether the Muse so wrought me from my birth,
Or I tomuch beleeued my shepherd peres)
Somedele ybent to song and musicks mirth,
A good olde shephearde, Wrenock was his name,
Made me by arte more cunning in the same.

Fro thence I durst in derring [doe] compare
With shepheards swayne, what euer fedde in field:
And if that Hobbinol right iudgement bare,

To Pan his owne selfe pype I neede not yield.
For if the flocking Nymphes did folow Pan,
The wiser Muses after Colin ranne.

But ah such pryde at length was ill repayde,
The shepheards God (perdie God was he none)
My hurtlesse pleasaunce did me ill vpbraide,
My freedome lorne, my life he lefte to mone.
Loue they him called, that gaue me checkmate,
But better mought they haue behote him Hate.

Tho gan my louely Spring bid me farewel,
And Sommer season sped him to display
(For loue then in the Lyons house did dwell)
The raging fyre, that kindled at his ray.
A comett stird vp that vnkindly heate,
That reigned (as men sayd) in Venus seate.

Forth was I ledde, not as I wont afore,
When choise I had to choose my wandring waye:
But whether luck and loues vnbridled lore
Would leade me forth on Fancies bitte to playe:
The bush my bedde, the bramble was my bowre,
The Woodes can witnesse many a wofull stowre.

Where I was wont to seeke the honey Bee,
Working her formall rowmes in Wexen frame:
The grieslie Todestool growne there mought I se
And loathed Paddocks lording on the same.
And where the chaunting birds luld me a sleepe,
The ghastlie Owle her grieuous ynne doth keepe.

Then as the springe giues place to elder time,
And bringeth forth the fruite of sommers pryde:
Also my age now passed yougthly pryme,
To thinges of ryper reason selfe applyed.
And learnd of lighter timber cotes to frame,
Such as might saue my sheepe and me fro shame.

To make fine cages for the Nightingale,
And Baskets of bulrushes was my wont:
Who to entrappe the fish in winding sale
Was better seene, or hurtful beastes to hont?
I learned als the signes of heauen to ken,
How Phoebe sayles, where Venus sittes and when.

And tryed time yet taught me greater thinges,
The sodain rysing of the raging seas:
The soothe of byrds by beating of their wings,
The power of herbs, both which can hurt and ease:
And which be wont tenrage the restlesse sheepe,
And which be wont to worke eternall sleepe.

But ah vnwise and witlesse Colin cloute,
That kydst the hidden kinds of many a wede:
Yet kydst not ene to cure thy sore hart roote,
Whose ranckling wound as yet does rifely bleede.
Why liuest thou stil, and yet hast thy deathes wound?
Why dyest thou stil, and yet aliue art founde?

Thus is my sommer worne away and wasted,
Thus is my haruest hastened all to rathe:
The eare that budded faire, is burnt & blasted,
And all my hoped gaine is turned to scathe.
Of all the seede, that in my youth was sowne,
Was nought but brakes and brambles to be mowne.

My boughes with bloosmes that crowned were at firste,
And promised of timely fruite such store,
Are left both bare and barrein now at erst:
The flattring fruite is fallen to grownd before.
And rotted, ere they were halfe mellow ripe:
My haruest wast, my hope away dyd wipe.

The fragrant flowres, that in my garden grewe,
Bene withered, as they had bene gathered long.
Theyr rootes bene dryed vp for lacke of dewe,
Yet dewed with teares they han be euer among.
Ah who has wrought my Ro[s]alind this spight
To spil the flowres, that should her girlond dight,

And I, that whilome wont to frame my pype,
Vnto the shifting of the shepheards foote:
Sike follies nowe haue gathered as too ripe,
And cast hem out, as rotten an vnsoote.
The loser Lasse I cast to please nomore,
One if I please, enough is me therefore.

And thus of all my haruest hope I haue
Nought reaped but a weedye crop of care:
Which, when I thought haue thresht in swelling sheaue,
Cockel for corne, and chaffe for barley bare.
Soone as the chaffe should in the fan be fynd,
All was blowne away of the wauering wynd.

So now my yeare drawes to his latter terme,
My spring is spent, my sommer burnt vp quite:
My harueste hasts to stirre vp winter sterne,
And bids him clayme with rigorous rage hys right.
So nowe he stormes with many a sturdy stoure,
So now his blustring blast eche coste doth scoure.

The carefull cold hath nypt my rugged rynde,
And in my face deepe furrowes eld hath pight:

My head besprent with hoary frost I fynd,
And by myne eie the Crow his clawe dooth wright.
Delight is layd abedde, and pleasure past,
No sonne now shines, cloudes han all ouercast.

Now leaue ye shepheards boyes yo[u]r merry glee,
My Muse is hoarse and weary of thys stounde:
Here will I hang my pype vpon this tree,
Was neuer pype of reede did better sounde.
Winter is come, that blowes the bitter blaste,
And after Winter dreerie death does hast.

Gather ye together my little flocke,
My little flock, that was to me so liefe:
Let me, ah lette me in your folds ye lock,
Ere the breme Winter breede you greater griefe.
Winter is come, that blowes the balefull breath,
And after Winter commeth timely death.

Adieu delightes, that lulled me asleepe,
Adieu my deare, whose loue I bought so deare:
Adieu my little Lambes and loued sheepe,
Adieu ye Woodes that oft my witnesse were:
Adieu good Hobbinol, that was so true,
Tell Rosalind, her Colin bids her adieu.

www.ingramcontent.com/pod-product-compliance
Lightning Source LLC
Chambersburg PA
CBHW071643050426
42443CB00026B/953